Planet Earth

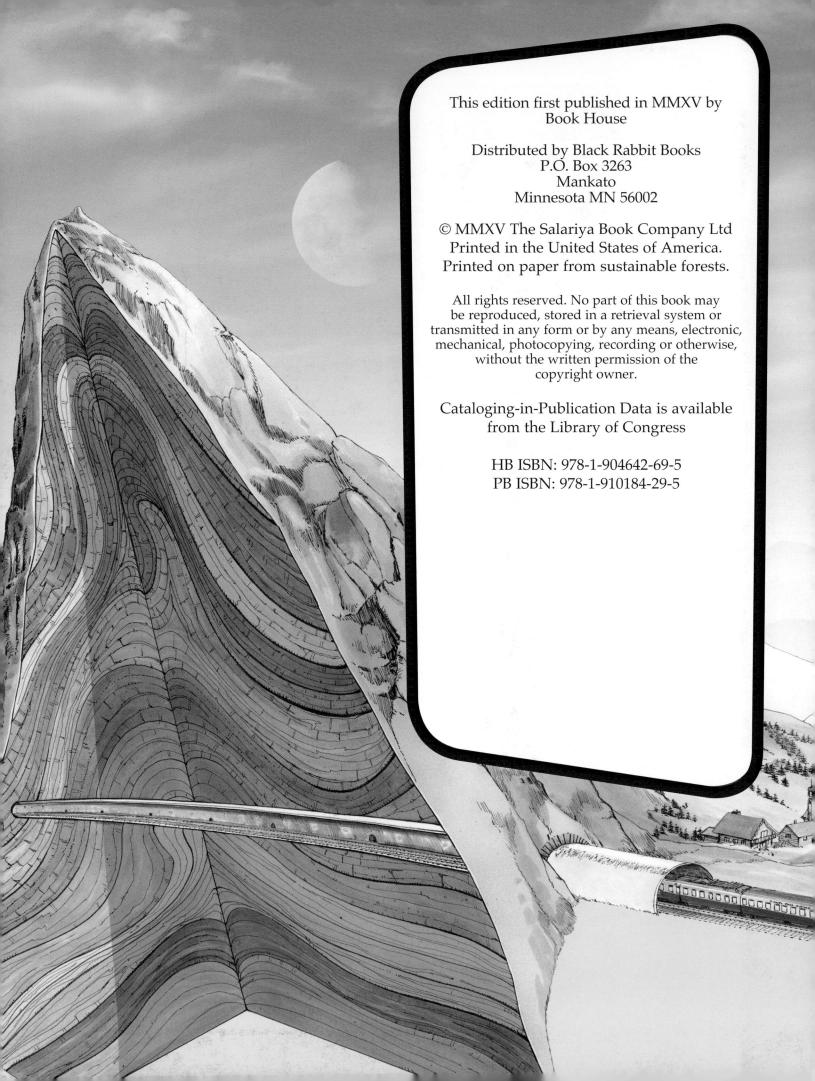

This edition first published in MMXV by
Book House

Distributed by Black Rabbit Books
P.O. Box 3263
Mankato
Minnesota MN 56002

© MMXV The Salariya Book Company Ltd
Printed in the United States of America.
Printed on paper from sustainable forests.

Cataloging-in-Publication Data is available
from the Library of Congress

HB ISBN: 978-1-904642-69-5
PB ISBN: 978-1-910184-29-5

A CLOSER LOOK AT

Planet Earth

Written by Margot Channing
Illustrated by Gerald Wood

CONTENTS

PLANET EARTH

Planet Earth is made up of a central core that is surrounded by two layers—a mantle and a thin outer crust. We see only the uppermost surface of Earth's outer crust—its mountains, oceans, rivers, and lakes. The upper part of Earth's mantle and its crust are made up of large rocky "plates." Powerful forces inside of Earth constantly exert pressure that moves these plates.

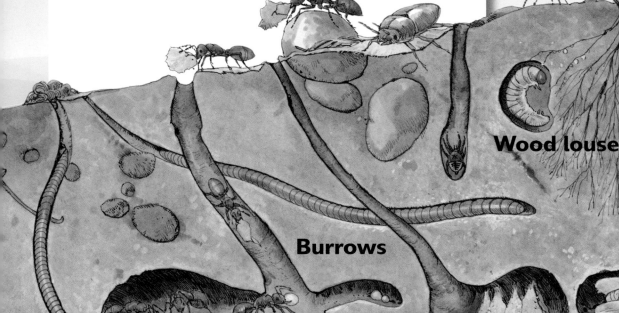

Ladybug

Wood louse

Burrows

Ant

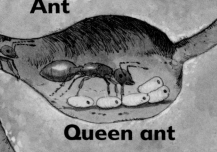

Soil is created by the wind, rain, and ice eroding Earth's rocky surface. Animals that burrow into the surface cause further erosion.

Queen ant

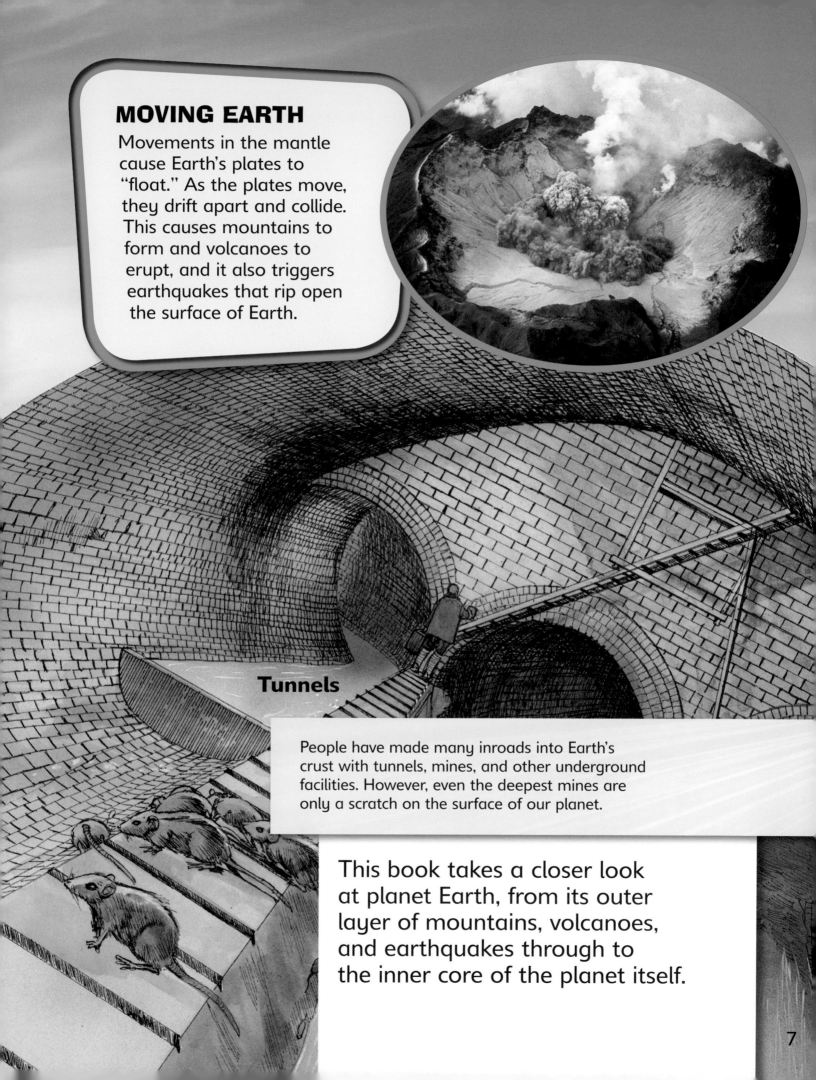

MOVING EARTH

Movements in the mantle cause Earth's plates to "float." As the plates move, they drift apart and collide. This causes mountains to form and volcanoes to erupt, and it also triggers earthquakes that rip open the surface of Earth.

Tunnels

People have made many inroads into Earth's crust with tunnels, mines, and other underground facilities. However, even the deepest mines are only a scratch on the surface of our planet.

This book takes a closer look at planet Earth, from its outer layer of mountains, volcanoes, and earthquakes through to the inner core of the planet itself.

MOUNTAINS

Mountain peak

Movement in Earth's plates creates mountains. Plates move very slowly—less than 4 in each year. However, over millions of years, the pressure of two plates pushing against each other can force the layers of rock between them into huge folds. This creates mountains.

THE ANDES AND ALPS

The plates beneath the Pacific Ocean and South America collided 150 million years ago. This created the Andes mountains. The Alps formed when the plate beneath Africa pushed into the plate beneath Europe about 26 million years ago.

Mountain climber

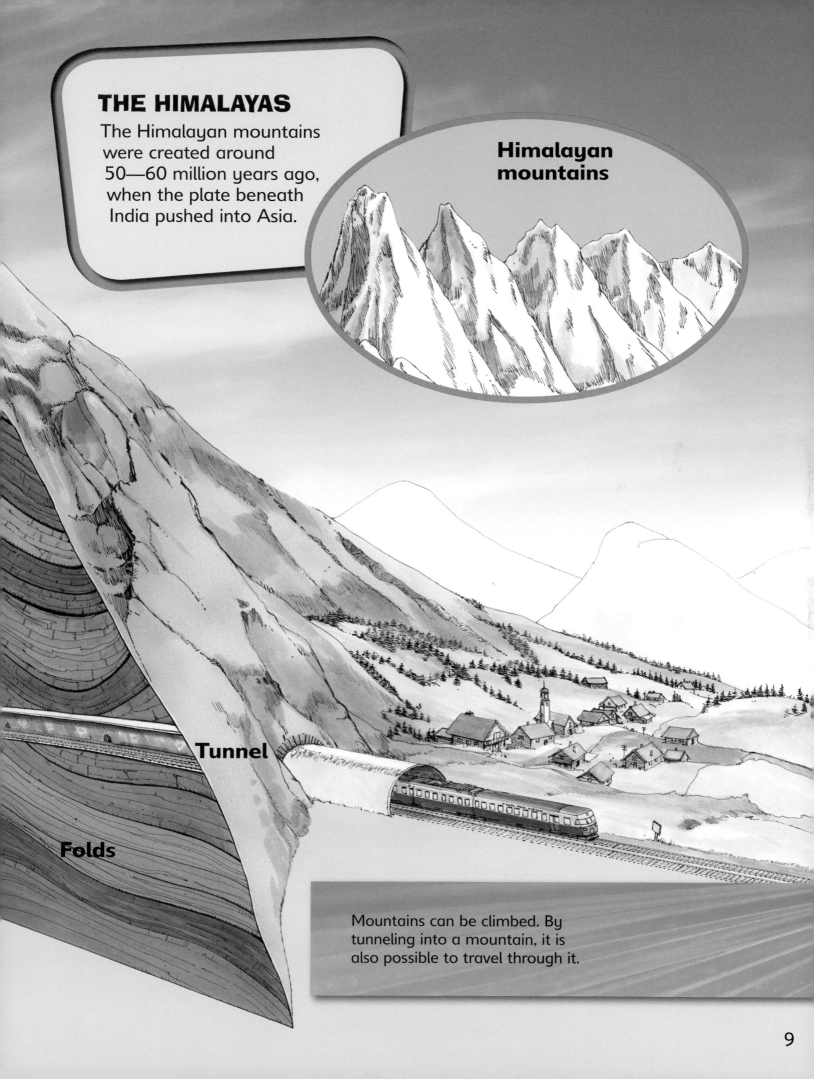

THE HIMALAYAS

The Himalayan mountains were created around 50—60 million years ago, when the plate beneath India pushed into Asia.

Himalayan mountains

Tunnel

Folds

Mountains can be climbed. By tunneling into a mountain, it is also possible to travel through it.

9

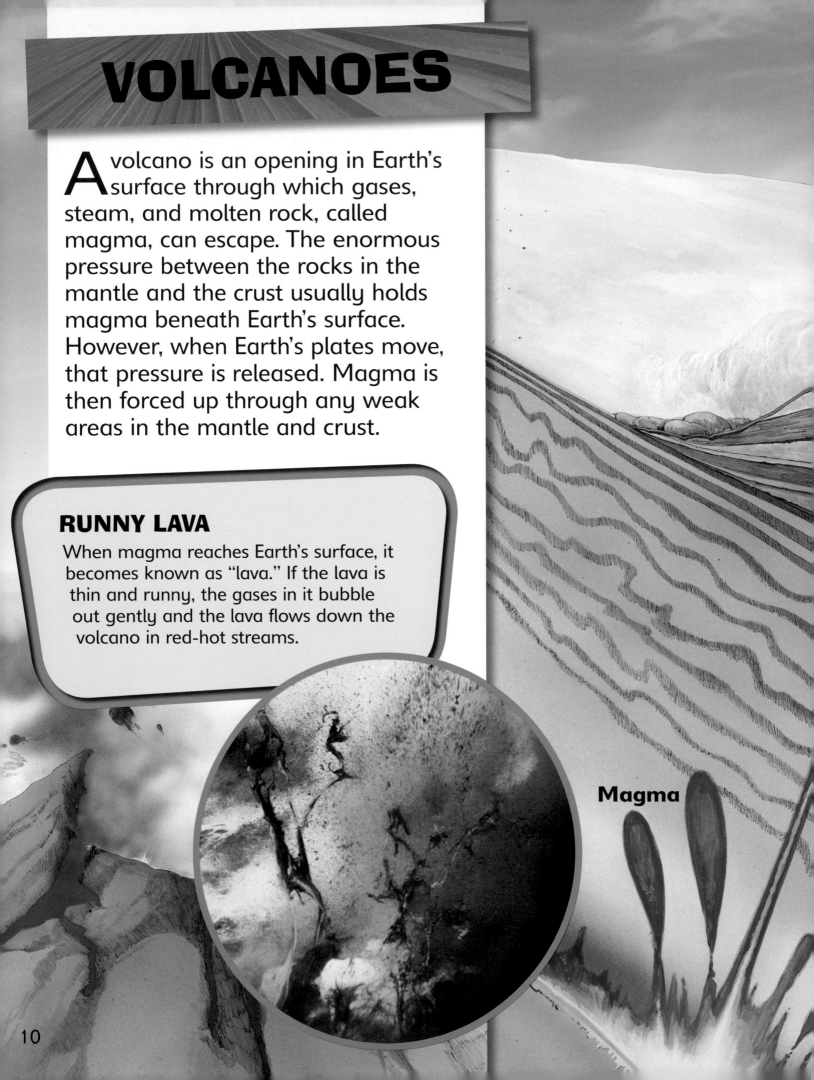

VOLCANOES

A volcano is an opening in Earth's surface through which gases, steam, and molten rock, called magma, can escape. The enormous pressure between the rocks in the mantle and the crust usually holds magma beneath Earth's surface. However, when Earth's plates move, that pressure is released. Magma is then forced up through any weak areas in the mantle and crust.

RUNNY LAVA

When magma reaches Earth's surface, it becomes known as "lava." If the lava is thin and runny, the gases in it bubble out gently and the lava flows down the volcano in red-hot streams.

Magma

Vent

THICK LAVA

If lava is thick and sticky, the gases inside it cannot escape. This causes a violent explosion. Bombs of lava are thrown into the sky, and huge clouds of ash, steam, and gas erupt from the volcano.

Magma flows up from the mantle through "fissures," or cracks, in Earth's crust. Magma reaches the surface though tubelike holes called "vents."

EARTHQUAKES

As plates slide past and beneath one another, an enormous pressure is created. Up to a point, the rock that forms Earth's crust can bend under the strain. However, when the pressure becomes too great, the rock snaps. The ground then shakes violently in what is known as an earthquake.

Earthquake destruction

EARTH'S VIBRATIONS

Vibrations in Earth's crust are known as "seismic waves." These vibrations are waves of energy that are generated by an earthquake and travel through Earth. Some seismic waves are so powerful, they can be felt hundreds of miles away.

Seismograph recording

CREATING AN EARTHQUAKE

1. A crack is formed in Earth's crust when areas of rock are pushed and pulled in opposite directions.

2. Over time, pressure in the crust builds up, and this weakened area starts to bend.

3. When the rock snaps, it shakes the ground. This causes an earthquake.

When earthquakes occur in large cities and towns, buildings often collapse and many people may die.

SOIL

When Earth first formed, around 4,600 million years ago, it was covered with incredibly hot rock. Slowly, the rock cooled and hardened. Rain, wind, and ice gradually eroded Earth's surface. Over time, the dead animals and plants that rotted into the surface of the planet formed soil.

LIVING IN SOIL

Many of the creatures and plants that live in soil are beneficial to it. Plant roots retain moisture and anchor the soil so that it is not blown or washed away.

Earthworm

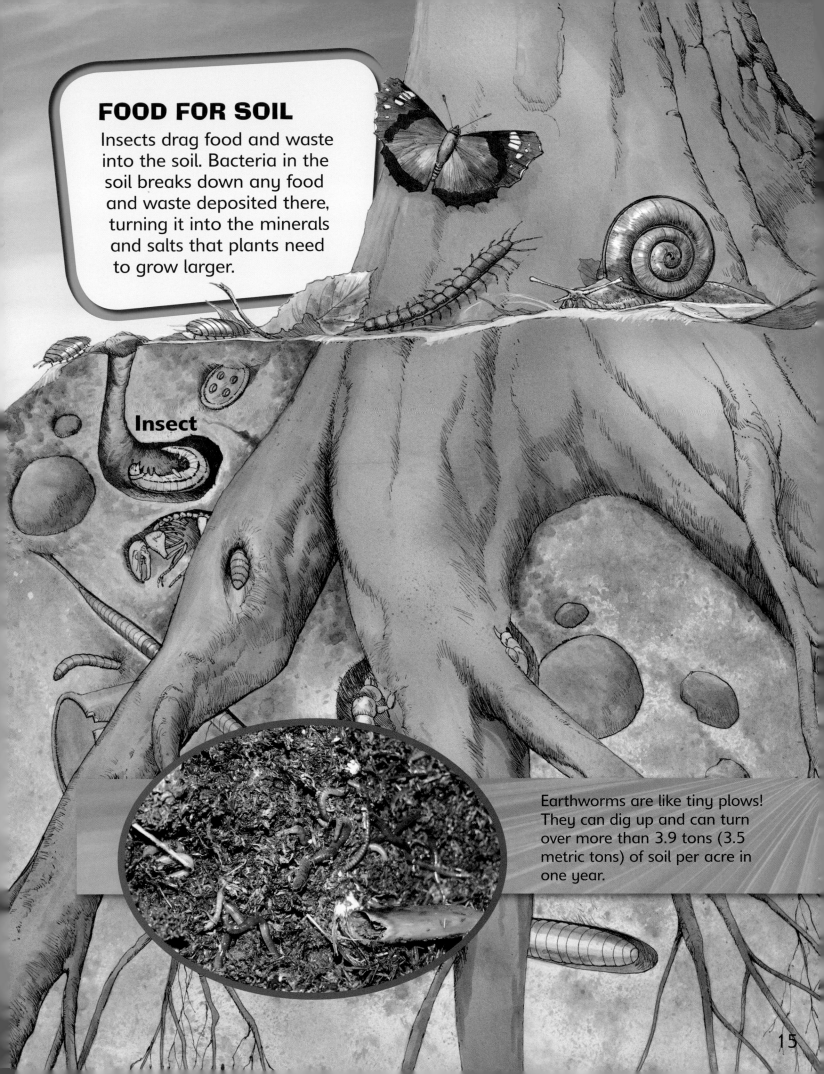

FOOD FOR SOIL

Insects drag food and waste into the soil. Bacteria in the soil breaks down any food and waste deposited there, turning it into the minerals and salts that plants need to grow larger.

Insect

Earthworms are like tiny plows! They can dig up and can turn over more than 3.9 tons (3.5 metric tons) of soil per acre in one year.

ANIMALS UNDERGROUND

The country may look peaceful, but below the ground, creatures are busy burrowing! Underground animals tunnel through the soil, looking for food. Many animals build their nests below ground. Burrowing animals help the soil by loosening it and letting in air and water.

PRECIOUS PONDS

Ponds are hollows in the ground that have filled with water. Like soil, ponds are homes for many plants and animals.

UNDERGROUND DIGGERS

Rabbits dig complex networks of tunnels that lead to underground chambers, or rooms. The networks and chambers are often reused by many generations of rabbits.

Tunnel network

Chamber

Moles spend most of their lives underground. They use their powerful front claws to dig through the soil, in search of food.

Mole

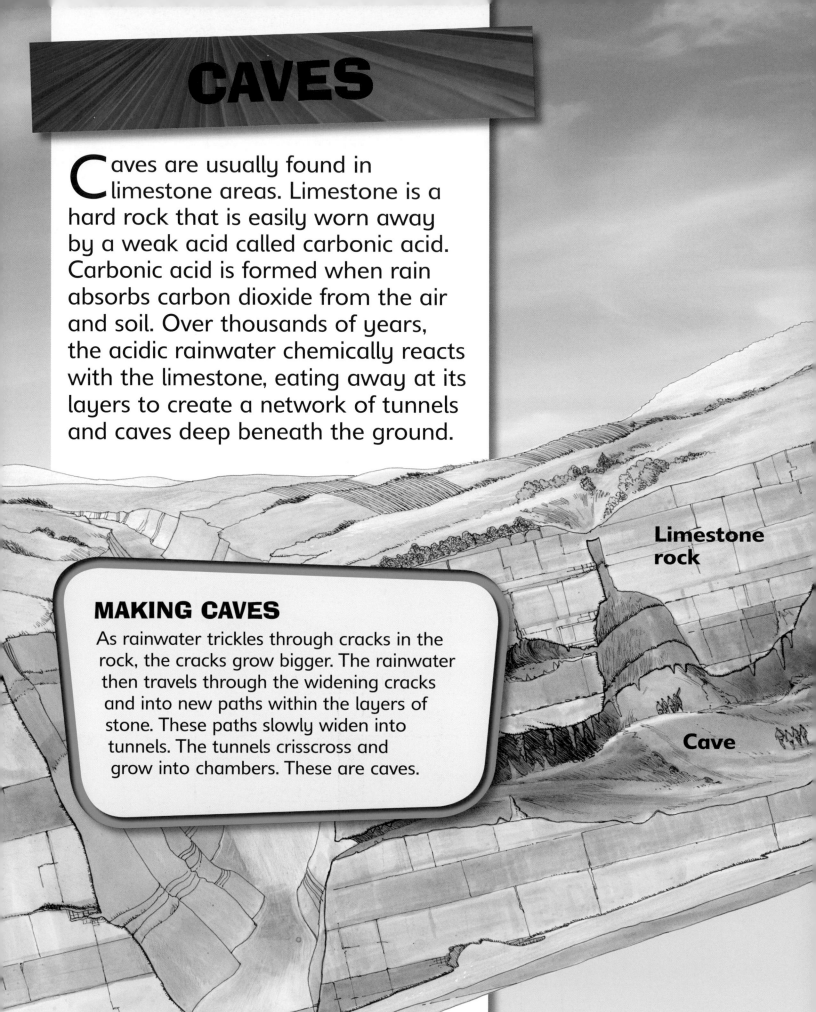

CAVES

Caves are usually found in limestone areas. Limestone is a hard rock that is easily worn away by a weak acid called carbonic acid. Carbonic acid is formed when rain absorbs carbon dioxide from the air and soil. Over thousands of years, the acidic rainwater chemically reacts with the limestone, eating away at its layers to create a network of tunnels and caves deep beneath the ground.

Limestone rock

Cave

MAKING CAVES

As rainwater trickles through cracks in the rock, the cracks grow bigger. The rainwater then travels through the widening cracks and into new paths within the layers of stone. These paths slowly widen into tunnels. The tunnels crisscross and grow into chambers. These are caves.

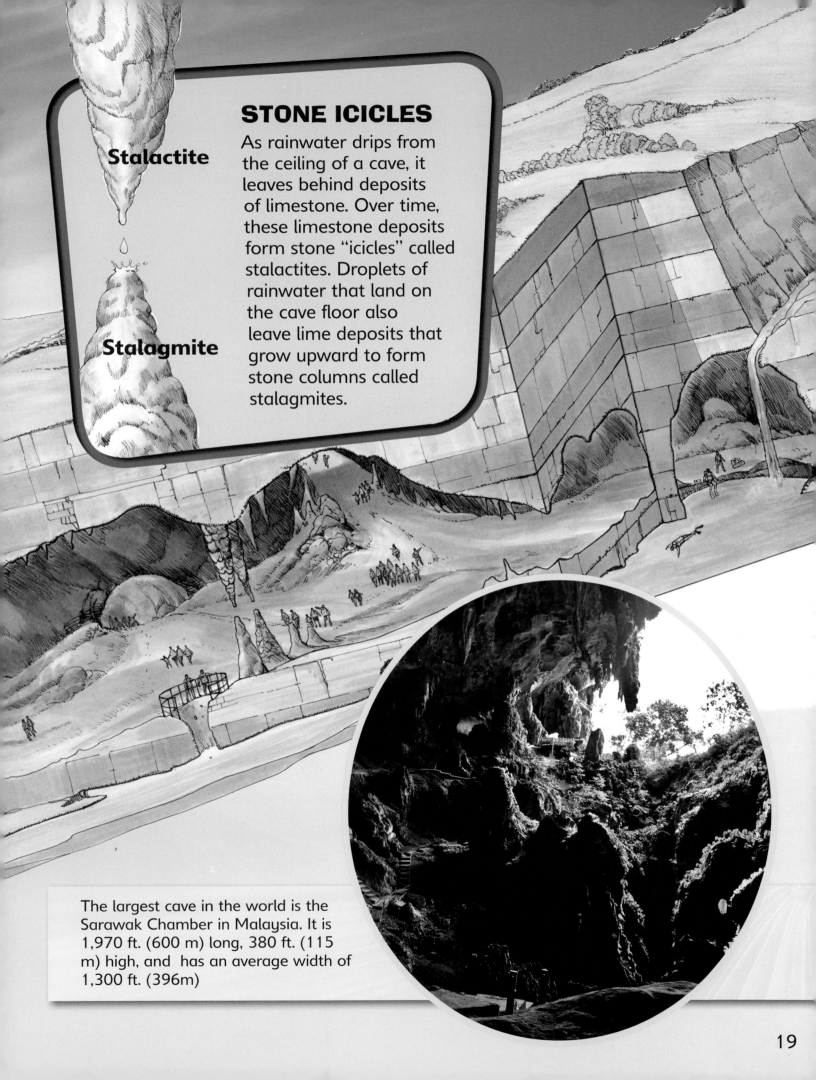

STONE ICICLES

Stalactite

Stalagmite

As rainwater drips from the ceiling of a cave, it leaves behind deposits of limestone. Over time, these limestone deposits form stone "icicles" called stalactites. Droplets of rainwater that land on the cave floor also leave lime deposits that grow upward to form stone columns called stalagmites.

The largest cave in the world is the Sarawak Chamber in Malaysia. It is 1,970 ft. (600 m) long, 380 ft. (115 m) high, and has an average width of 1,300 ft. (396m)

TUNNELS

People first began to dig tunnels in the ground in order to mine gold and tin, among other things. Tunnels were also dug to reach underground water sources. Several hundred years ago, the ancient Greeks and Romans dug amazing tunnels. Today, we have power drills, digging machines, and explosives to help us build tunnels beneath Earth's surface.

CUT AND COVER TUNNELS

The quickest way that we build tunnels today is by digging a deep trench in the ground and lining the sides with solid walls. A roof is then built, and the entire structure is covered with soil and rock. This method of tunneling is called "cut and cover."

Tunneling machine used for underground train tunnel construction

TUNNELING MACHINES

We use tunneling machines to dig tunnels. The machine moves forward slowly, cutting into the rock with rotating blades. The broken rock is carried away on a conveyor belt.

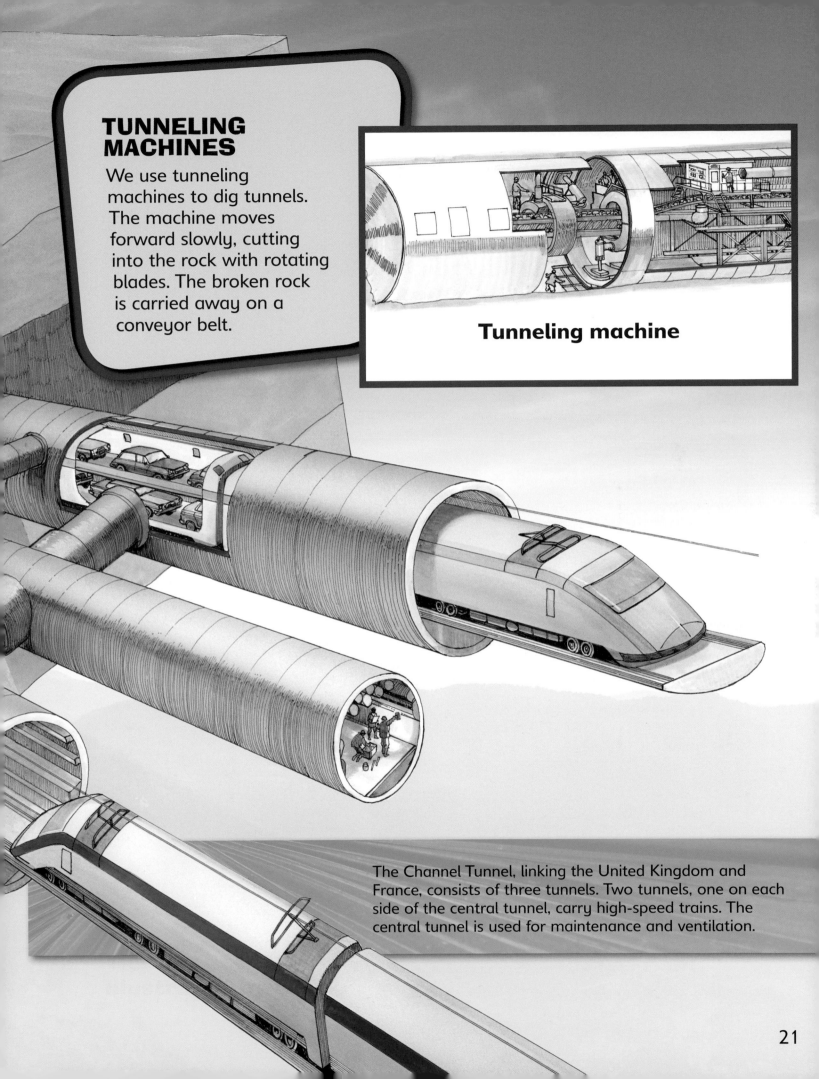

Tunneling machine

The Channel Tunnel, linking the United Kingdom and France, consists of three tunnels. Two tunnels, one on each side of the central tunnel, carry high-speed trains. The central tunnel is used for maintenance and ventilation.

CABLES, DRAINS, AND SEWERS

People rarely travel beyond the upper layer of Earth's surface. However, the buildings we live and work in rely on a network of underground facilities. Beneath the streets of any modern city is a system of cables, drains, and sewers.

WATER SUPPLY

When we turn on a faucet, water flows. It has been transported from our local reservoirs through water mains. Water mains are special pipes that carry water beneath our cities' streets. Drains take away wastewater and carry it into a sewer system.

Drain

Rats that live in underground sewers and tunnels can cause chaos. They sometimes bite through cables and pipes.

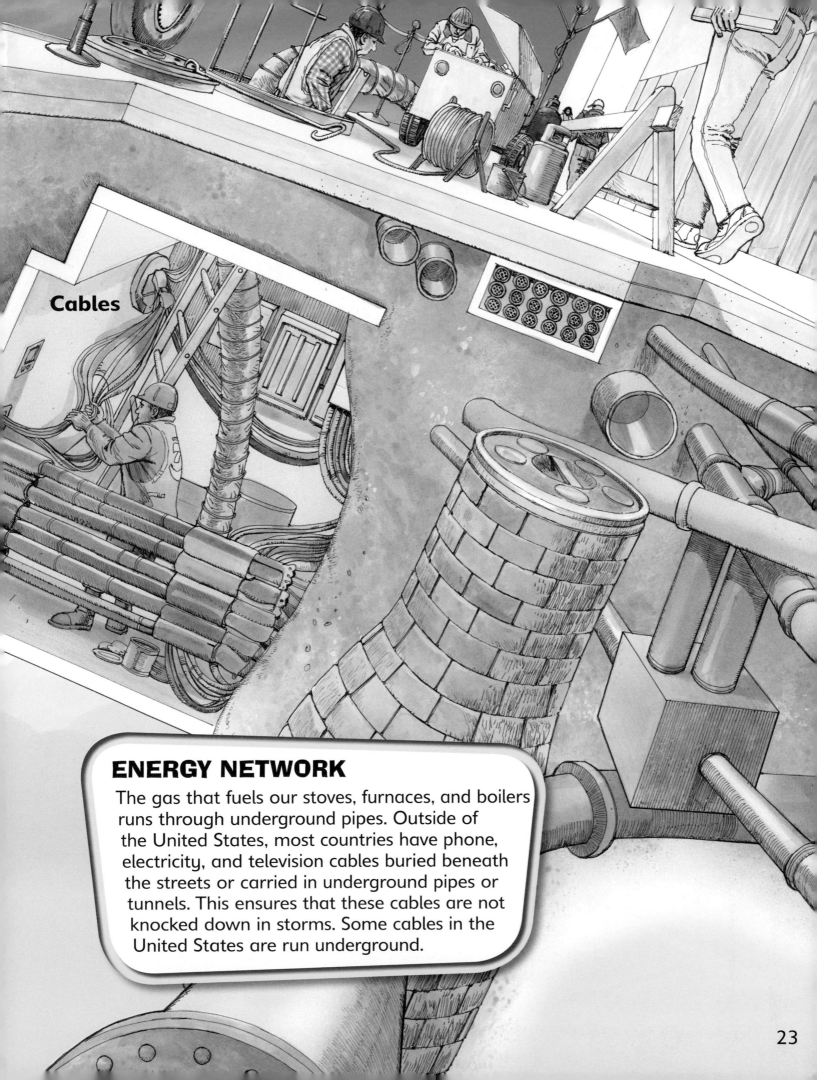

Cables

ENERGY NETWORK

The gas that fuels our stoves, furnaces, and boilers runs through underground pipes. Outside of the United States, most countries have phone, electricity, and television cables buried beneath the streets or carried in underground pipes or tunnels. This ensures that these cables are not knocked down in storms. Some cables in the United States are run underground.

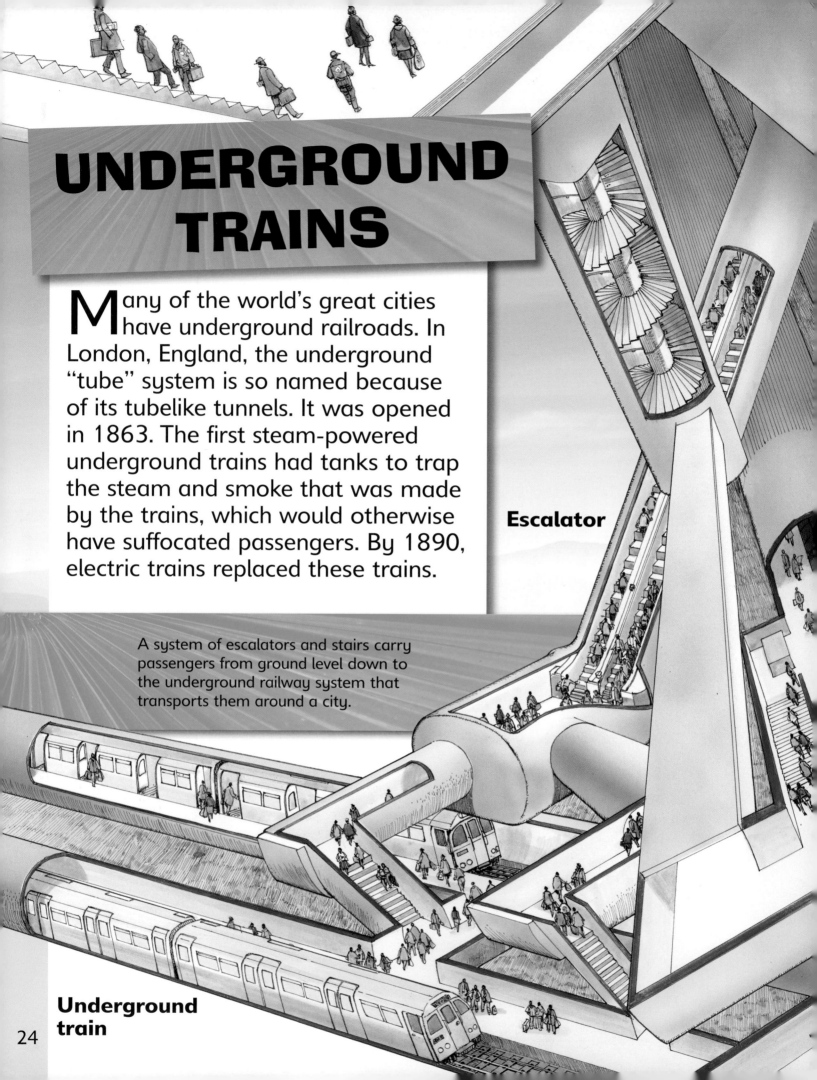

UNDERGROUND TRAINS

Many of the world's great cities have underground railroads. In London, England, the underground "tube" system is so named because of its tubelike tunnels. It was opened in 1863. The first steam-powered underground trains had tanks to trap the steam and smoke that was made by the trains, which would otherwise have suffocated passengers. By 1890, electric trains replaced these trains.

Escalator

A system of escalators and stairs carry passengers from ground level down to the underground railway system that transports them around a city.

Underground train

RUSH HOUR

Today, underground train systems carry passengers around cities throughout the day and, sometimes, the night. This underground travel system helps reduce the amount of traffic on the streets above.

NEW YORK CITY AND PARIS

New York City has a system of railroad tunnels called the "subway." Paris has a system called the "metro."

25

MINES

Earth's rocky surface is made up of minerals. A mineral is a substance that is found in nature but that is neither a plant nor an animal. Minerals include metals such as copper, gold, and tin. Minerals have been mined since ancient times. One of the most valuable of all is coal.

Coal mine

MAKING COAL

Coal is formed from the remains of trees and other plants that lived millions of years ago. When the plants and trees died, they fell into swamps. There, they decayed into a black material called peat. As moisture was pressed out over many years, the peat turned into coal.

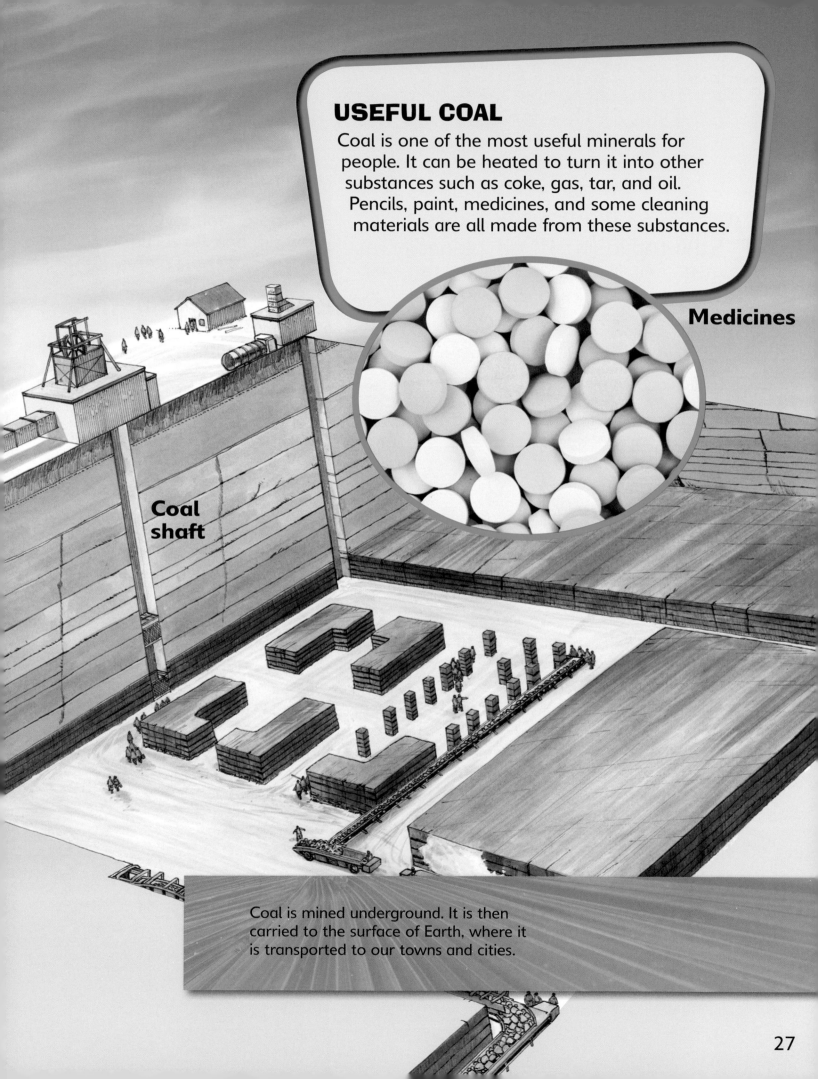

USEFUL COAL

Coal is one of the most useful minerals for people. It can be heated to turn it into other substances such as coke, gas, tar, and oil. Pencils, paint, medicines, and some cleaning materials are all made from these substances.

Medicines

Coal shaft

Coal is mined underground. It is then carried to the surface of Earth, where it is transported to our towns and cities.

TOWARD THE CORE

All life on Earth exists within the top layers of the planet's crust. Even the deepest mines created by humans descend only a short distance into the crust. We cannot yet travel deep within Earth, but we are finding out more and more about it with the use of scientific equipment. In years to come, our incredible planet will reveal many more of its amazing secrets.

HOW DEEP?

We now know that Earth's crust can be between 2—25 miles (3—40 km) thick. Earth's mantle, between the crust and outer core, can be around 1,800 miles (2,900 km) deep. The liquid outer core is around 1,240 miles (2,000 km) thick, and Earth's inner core is around 850 miles (1,370 km) thick.

Earth's core

Earth's rocky surface

HOW HOT?

At 250 miles (400 km) below Earth's surface, the temperature is around 2,500 °F (1,370 °C). Its core, at the center of Earth, may be as hot as 10,800 °F (6,000 °C). There, the forces that have shaped our planet for millions of years are still red-hot.

Part of Earth's mantle is still made up of magma. Magma rises up and collects in a magma chamber in the upper layer of the mantle. It then forces its way into weak spots in Earth's crust.

Magma chamber

GLOSSARY

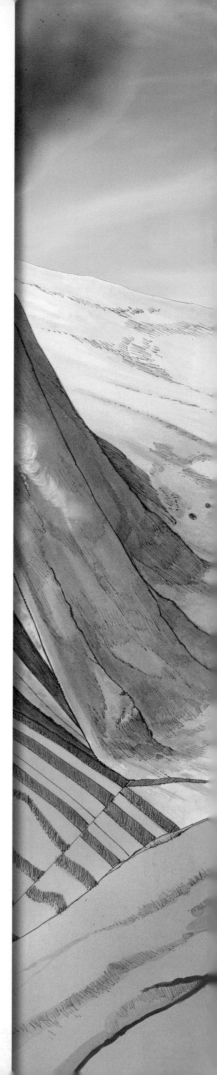

Bacteria microscopic, single-celled organisms found in soil, water, and air. Many types of bacteria cause chemical changes, such as the decay of dead plants and animals.

Carbon dioxide a colorless, odorless gas that is heavier than air.

Carbonic acid a weak, colorless acid that forms when carbon dioxide is dissolved in water.

Core Earth's core is made up of two parts—a liquid outer core and a solid inner core. The core reaches from the deepest part of the mantle to the center of Earth, a distance of 2,100 miles (3,370 km).

Crust the thin outer layer of Earth. Its thickness varies from just 2 miles (3 km) under the oceans to as much as 50 miles (80 km) under mountains.

Erosion the wearing away of land by weathering, running water, ice, and winds.

Fissure a long crack through which gas and magma find their way to Earth's surface.

Insect a small animal with six legs, two or four wings, and a body divided into three sections.

Lava molten rock that flows onto Earth's surface.

Limestone a rock that was formed millions of years ago. Some limestone was formed when tiny sea animals died and fell to the bottom of the sea. There, they formed a soft layer. Over time, the layer was covered with other deposits. When it hardened, it formed limestone.

Magma molten rock inside Earth. When magma reaches Earth's surface, it is called lava.

Mantle Earth's mantle extends beyond the crust to a depth of around 1,800 miles (2,900 km). It is mostly solid but contains some partially liquid rock.

Mineral a substance that occurs naturally on Earth.

Molten melted, as in molten rock called magma.

Planet one of the eight bodies that revolve around the Sun. Earth is one of these planets.

Plate one of the several large rocky areas that make up Earth's surface.

Reservoir a large lake in which water is collected and stored.

Seismic waves vibrations caused by an earthquake.

Sewer a tunnel that carries dirty water and human waste.

Tunnel an underground passage.

Volcano an opening in Earth's surface through which magma, gases, and steam can escape. Mountains that form around such openings are also called volcanoes.

INDEX